SIMPLE MACHINES

screws

VALERIE BODDEN

Published by Creative Education
P.O. Box 227, Mankato, Minnesota 56002
Creative Education is an imprint of The Creative Company
www.thecreativecompany.us

Design and production by Liddy Walseth
Art direction by Rita Marshall
Printed by Corporate Graphics in the United States of America

Photographs by Alamy (Goss Images), Dreamstime (Sarah Fields, Liubomir
Turcanu), Getty Images (Peter Adams, J Jay Hirz/Archive Photos, Adam Jones,
Richard Laird, Oxford Scientific/Photolibrary, Greg Pease, Justin Pumfrey,
Ed Reeve, Dominique Sarraute, Harry Sieplinga/HMS Images), iStockphoto
(Kirby Hamilton, Alan Heartfield, Daniela Jovanovska-Hristovska, Alex Kotlov)

Library of Congress Cataloging-in-Publication Data
Bodden, Valerie.
Screws / by Valerie Bodden.
p. cm. — (Simple machines)
Summary: A foundational look at screws, explaining how these simple machines
work and describing some common examples, such as jar lids, that have been
used throughout history.
Includes index.
ISBN 978-1-60818-011-0
1. Screws—Juvenile literature. I. Title. II. Series.
TJ1338.B593 2011
621.8'82—dc22 2009048860
CPSIA: 040110 PO1140

First Edition
2 4 6 8 9 7 5 3 1

CREATIVE ◖ EDUCATION

SIMPLE MACHINES

screws

VALERIE BODDEN

contents

Have you ever turned a lid on a jar or walked up a spiral (*SPY-rul*) staircase? You might not have known it, but you were using a screw. A screw makes it easier to FASTEN or lift objects.

A screw
does not
have any
moving
parts

A screw is a kind of simple machine. Simple machines have only a few moving parts. Some have no moving parts at all. Simple machines help people do WORK.

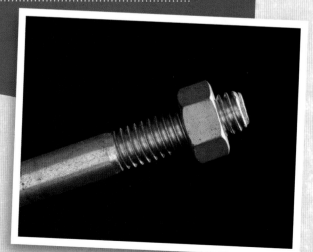

A screw is a pole with an INCLINED PLANE wrapped around it. The inclined plane looks like a line that winds up the pole of the screw. The line is called a thread.

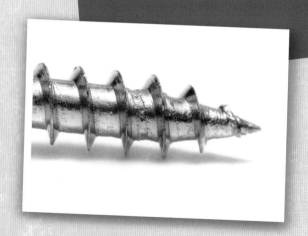

Screws that are used to fasten things together are not hammered into objects like nails. Instead, they are usually turned with a screwdriver. As the screw is turned, the thread helps pull it farther into the object.

On some screws, the lines of the thread are close together. This makes the screws easier to turn. On other screws, the lines of the thread are far apart.

These screws are harder to turn. But you do not have to turn them as many times to fasten them to an object.

A tool
called a
wrench
can tighten
some screws

Sometimes screws are used with NUTS. The inside of a nut has a thread that fits with the thread of the screw. The nut holds the screw in place.

Screws used in old wine-presses are huge

People have been using screws for thousands of years. About 2,000 years ago, big screws were used to press boards together in WINEPRESSES. Later, screws made out of metal were used with screwdrivers.

People still use screws today. Screws hold buildings, furniture, and machines together. Even the lid of a jar is a screw. So is the bottom of a light bulb!

A spiral staircase is a type of screw

Screws can help lift heavy objects, too. A car JACK has a screw that turns to lift a car off the ground. Screws are everywhere. Without them, we would have a much harder time lifting and fastening the objects around us!

A CLOSER LOOK at *Screws*

YOU CAN SEE HOW WELL A SCREW FASTENS OBJECTS BY FILLING A CLEAN, EMPTY PEANUT BUTTER JAR WITH SAND. SCREW THE COVER ON TIGHTLY, AND TIP THE JAR UPSIDE DOWN. SHAKE IT. WHAT HAPPENS? TRY THE SAME THING WITH THE COVER SCREWED ON LOOSELY. DOES IT HOLD THE SAND AS WELL? NOW PUSH THE COVER ONTO THE JAR WITHOUT TURNING IT. TIP THE JAR UPSIDE DOWN ONE MORE TIME. WHAT HAPPENS?

Glossary

fasten—to hold two or more objects together

inclined plane—a simple machine made up of a flat surface that is higher at one end than the other

jack—a machine that lifts heavy objects such as cars a short distance off the ground

nuts—small pieces of metal with a hole in the middle; there is a thread on the inside of the hole

winepresses—machines used to squeeze the juice out of grapes

work—using force (a push or pull) to move an object

Read More

Oxlade, Chris. *Screws.* Chicago: Heinemann Library, 2003.

Thales, Sharon. *Screws to the Rescue.* Mankato, Minn.: Capstone Press, 2007.

Web Sites

MIKIDS.com

http://www.mikids.com/Smachines.htm

Learn about the six kinds of simple machines and see examples of each one.

Simple Machines

http://staff.harrisonburg.k12.va.us/~mwampole/1-resources/simple-machines/index.html

Try to figure out which common objects are simple machines.

Index